COMPOSTING
Made
EASY

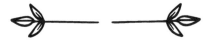

Beginner's Guide to Quickly and Effortlessly Composting Kitchen Waste, Even in Your Apartment | Boost Productivity and Soil Health Naturally

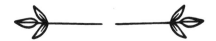

Jacob A. Moore

© Copyright 2022 by Jacob A. Moore - All rights reserved.

All rights reserved. No part of this book may be reproduced in any form without permission in writing from the author. Reviewers may quote brief passages in reviews.

While all attempts have been made to verify the information provided in this publication, neither the author nor the publisher assumes any responsibility for errors, omissions, or contrary interpretation of the subject matter herein.

The views expressed in this publication are those of the author alone and should not be taken as expert instruction or commands. The reader is responsible for his or her own actions, as well as his or her own interpretation of the material found within this publication.

Adherence to all applicable laws and regulations, including international, federal, state and local governing professional licensing, business practices, advertising, and all other aspects of doing business in the US, Canada or any other jurisdiction is the sole responsibility of the reader and consumer.

Neither the author nor the publisher assumes any responsibility or liability whatsoever on behalf of the consumer or reader of this material. Any perceived slight of any individual or organization is purely unintentional.

TABLE OF CONTENT

INTRODUCTION 7
BENEFITS OF COMPOSTING 11
CHEMISTRY AND MICROORGANISMS 15
Chemistry Behind Composting 16
Composting Parameters 18
Hot Composting Vs Cold Composting 19
How To Make Hot Compost 21
Aerobic Vs. Anaerobic 22
Benign Bacteria, Microorganisms And Molds 24

WHAT TO COMPOST 27
Compostable Materials To Pay Attention To 28
What not to compost 30

COMPOSTING METHODS 33
Trench Composting 33
    Benefits of trench composting 34
    Disadvantages of trench composting 35
    Equipment required 35
    Start-up & maintenance procedure: 36
Pile Composting 37
    Benefits of pile composting 38
    Disadvantages of pile composting 39
    Equipment required 39
    Start-up & maintenance procedure 40
Tumbler Composting 41
    Benefits of tumbler composting: 41
    Disadvantages of tumbler composting: 42
    Equipment required 43

Start-up & maintenance procedure 43

Worm Composting 47
Benefits of worm composting 47
Disadvantages of worm composting 48
Equipment required 49
Start up & maintenance 49

Bin Composting 53
Benefits of bin composting: 54
Disadvantages of bin composting: 54
Start up & maintenance: 54

Bokashi Composting 56
Advantages of bokashi composting 57
Disadvantages of bokashi composting 58
Start up & maintenance 58

Composting Machine 59
Advantages of composting machines: 61
Disadvantages of composting machines 63
Start up & maintenance 64

COMPOST GATHERING AND USAGE 67
How To Tell If Compost Is Mature 67
How To Use Compost 68
How To Store Compost 71
Compost Tea 72
All the benefits: 73
How to make compost tea 74
How To Use Compost Tea 75

HOW TO SPEED UP THE COMPOSTING PROCESS 77
How To Prepare & Use The Compost Accelerator 78
How The DIY Compost Accelerator Works 79
Proper Usage 80

MAKE MONEY WITH COMPOST 83

The Benefits Of Composting Business: 83
The Disadvantages Of Composting Business: 85
How to Start Your Composting Business 86
    1)   Plan your business.. 86
    2)   Choose a location... 88
    3)   Find sources of organic waste... 89
    4)   Choose a composting method and build your farm............................ 90
    5)   Sell your product.. 91

TROUBLESHOOTING 93

My Compost Is Too Wet 93
My Compost Is Too Dry 94
My Compost Is Too Acid 95
My Compost Smells 95
My Compost Is Not Aerated 96
My Compost Is Crawling With Insects 97
    Insect management in compost.. 98
My Compost Attracts Animals 102

COMPOSTING FOR KIDS 103

Composting Projects For Kids 107
    Treasure hunts... 107
    Mini plastic composter.. 108
    Build a worm farm... 110

CONCLUSION 112

INTRODUCTION

Have you ever wondered if there was a way to provide utility to the waste you naturally produce? If the answer is yes, then this is the right book. Every time we eat we also produce organic waste that could make compost: fruit peels, vegetable scraps, food scraps, shells, coffee grounds. The times in which we live require us to do some important thinking, both about how to minimize waste in the kitchen and how to make the most of all that waste we inevitably produce. Let's see together what you can do concretely.

Differentiating waste correctly is the crucial first step. What may seem to us to be an insignificant daily action hides a power and strength that, multiplied for each of us, can make all the difference. Careful recycling collection helps us reduce waste and the negative impacts associated with disposal, while facilitating the recovery of materials. By recycling we avoid the consumption of new raw materials and save energy in their production.

Remember that just as materials such as paper, glass, plastic or aluminum are recycled to give them a second life, in the same way organic waste can be turned into a new material: compost. Anything that has been living, that is, has an animal or plant origin, can be composted:

- Organic scraps and leftovers: Fruit and vegetable peels, meat and pasta scraps, tea or coffee grounds, egg shells;

- Garden and vegetable garden waste: Dry leaves, small prunings, herbs, flowers;
- Any certified biodegradable and compostable product.

Composting is an all-natural biological process by which organic materials (twigs, grass, flowers, fruit and vegetable remains, etc.), chopped up, mixed and aerated to ensure adequate oxygenation, decompose through the action of microorganisms, earthworms and insects, transforming into humus-rich soil that can be used to replenish nutrients and bioelements in the soil. Composting therefore is useful both for ensuring soil fertility and for reducing the amount of waste going to landfills. The benefits increase when one considers that compost is a natural, environmentally friendly fertilizer that can at least partially replace chemical fertilizers and eliminate or reduce the use of other soils and substrates. Composting can be done by means of the appropriate compost bin or, if you have sufficient space and have large amounts of organic waste to recycle, through the formation of a heap.

Compost is a valuable resource as it enriches the soil with organic matter that gradually releases nutrients of fundamental importance to plants such as phosphorus, nitrogen and potassium. It also makes the soil structure more porous, increasing its ability to breathe and hold water, reducing the risk of flooding, and then slowly releasing it to the plants that need it. It also increases the filtering capacity of rainwater, promoting the supply of clean water from aquifers. Adding compost to soil supports life and biodiversity because it provides a better habitat for soil organisms. Finally, it is an effective means of sequestering carbon from the atmosphere by storing it in the soil (carbon farming), thus reducing the greenhouse effect. All these characteristics make compost not only an excellent natural fertilizer, suitable for a wide variety of uses in agriculture, but also a versatile and very powerful tool for combating climate change.

Enjoy your read,

Jacob A. Moore

BENEFITS OF COMPOSTING

Many times, rather than resorting to chemical and synthetics products, going back to the old homemade remedies is the best solution. Such is the case with home composting, which, with minimal effort, provides something that can prove vital for all green spaces. Many people think that composting is nothing more than an environmentally sustainable way to reduce and reuse household waste *(the kind we would normally throw in the wet waste)*. True, limiting waste is a good habit but compost brings great benefits to the garden as it has a large number of interesting features. *What exactly does it do?* Let's look at it together.

Improves soil quality

The use of compost can help improve soil health and replace, at least in part, the use of pesticides and chemical fertilizers by reducing reliance on other soils, thereby improving farmers' productivity and incomes. Healthy soil is usually a rich brown color, is soft to the touch and crumbly. These characteristics indicate that the right amount of air and moisture is circulating in it and it has enough space to move freely. Adding compost to the soil will help it get to this optimal situation and keep it healthy for the future. It also helps balance the pH of the soil, which is very helpful in allowing plants to grow beautiful and lush.

Reducing waste

Large amounts of organic material are still sent to landfills or incineration instead of being returned to farmland after the composting process. This results in high environmental, economic and social costs because organic waste in landfills can become very hazardous, producing leachates that can end up in groundwater with negative effects on human health and climate. In addition, organic matter in landfills produces methane, a very potent greenhouse gas that, if released into the atmosphere, has very negative effects on the climate. So with composting we will have helped to reduce garbage and improve the waste disposal chain. Which is something we greatly need.

Saving on fertilizer usage

Compost is the best fertilizer offered by nature. It is essentially a collection of organisms that live in the soil: bacteria and fungi and other common garden creatures, such as earthworms. These organisms help the soil stay healthy, plus the organic matter found in compost allows essential nutrients to be more easily retained in the soil and then used by plants and outside to grow. The use of compost can help improve soil health and largely replace the use of pesticides and chemical fertilizers by reducing reliance on other soils, thereby improving farmers' productivity and incomes. In addition, by improving the soil's ability to retain water, it increases its resistance to periods of drought, erosion and desertification. It also improves the soil's filtering capacity against excess pollutants and fertilizers, ensuring cleaner water in our aquifers;

Environmental impact

Carbon is the main component of soil organic matter, accounting for 58 percent of it. Increasing soil organic matter through the use of compost helps sequester carbon dioxide from the atmosphere, reducing the greenhouse effect in the short to medium term. More generally, by reducing waste, composting also helps reduce greenhouse gas emissions that affect climate change.

Keeps garden diseases in check

Recent studies show that compost helps keep your garden's most harmful pests at bay. While the most barren soils can easily be invaded by them, compost will naturally reduce the number of these problem pests, keeping your garden beautiful and healthy. Compost is also great for keeping the soil the right consistency, consequently making it easier to manage. Soil compaction can be a problem if it is dry. It also helps stop erosion, and if you have clay soil in your garden, it can facilitate drainage and aeration.

So far we have seen what compost is, the benefits, use cases, and how starting this practice can make a concrete difference. As consumers and citizens, we can be instrumental in sorting household wet waste by remembering that certified biodegradable and compostable manufactured goods and packaging can also be disposed of in the same container. Every time we sort, we actively help the community to reduce the amount of waste to be disposed of while contributing to a more efficient use of resources, with both environmental and economic benefits. The valorization of organic waste, through composting, allows us to obtain a valuable material such as compost that does not waste resources and contributes to decreasing our impact on the environment.

CHEMISTRY AND MICROORGANISMS

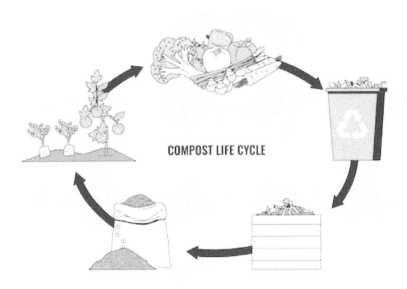

So how can compost be obtained? And what are the processes that lead to it? Basically, composting is a process of aerobic digestion of organic material in waste; this process is carried out by the various types of microorganisms (*bacteria, fungi, protozoa*) naturally present in the environment. These microorganisms degrade the organic substances present in waste and transform them into simpler substances; this is because they derive energy from the processes of degradation of these substances; in addition, many types of bacteria are able to store energy in the form of polymers of various types, again from aerobic digestion (*e.g., polyhydroxybutyrate, PHB*). But in order to do this, these microorganisms need oxygen, i.e., the process must take place in an aerobic environment; in addition, a whole series of parameters must be present to allow the development and growth of the microorganisms *(pH, temperature, water, nitrogen, etc.)*; the end result is the so-called humus, i.e., a mix of organic substances constituting compost.

Chemistry Behind Composting

These substances are better known as humic acid, fulvic acid and humin, each of which is a family of substances; the elemental composition of most humic substances is within the following ranges:

C 45-55%; O 30-45%; H 3-6%; N 1-5%; S 0-1%.

In more detail, they are high-molecular-weight polyelectrolyte macromolecules that have the ability to bind metal ions. The composting process can basically be divided into 2 phases:

1) a bio-oxidation phase, characterized by moderately high temperatures (up to about 140°F) resulting from microbial activity (fresh compost);

2) a maturation phase, where the transformation of organic substances into humic substances takes place (mature compost).

The first phase is an aerobic and exothermic process: this is because there is an intense microbial activity favored by the availability of fermentable raw materials (sugars, amino acids, fatty acids) and atmospheric oxygen, and part of the energy is dissipated in the form of heat; in addition, in this phase the sanitization of the compost takes place due to the high temperatures reached (over 140°F), thus destroying any pathogenic germs.

The result of this first phase is the production of fresh compost and some simple substances *(CO_2, water, NH_3, sulfur compounds)* and acidic in character *(short-chain carboxylic acids such as acetic acid or propionic acid)* and subsequent lowering of the pH. Once the simpler compounds to be degraded are exhausted, the microbial population undergoes a change, due to the lack of nutrients: thus, fungi and actinomycetes begin to develop, which start to degrade the more complex substances *(lignin, starch, cellulose)* resulting in a slowdown of the processes and progressive lowering of the temperature, until the mature compost is obtained, dark in color, rich in humic substances and with a characteristic smell of forest loam.

Humus is a fundamental reservoir of nutrients for plants, as it is capable of constantly releasing into the soil the nutrients that are essential for them, such as nitrogen, phosphorus, sulfur, calcium, iron, potassium, etc.; these elements are retained by humic macromolecules *(for example: metals)* and absorbed by the plant if necessary, or produced by the mineralization of humic substances by microorganisms. However, microorganisms necessarily need an ideal environment in which to proliferate and degrade organic substances; in other words, their activity is influenced by a whole series of physical and chemical parameters, which are crucial in the case of industrial composting.

Composting Parameters

The temperature is the parameter that gives useful information about the progress of the process: in the first phase, as already mentioned, the temperature is higher and through the action of thermophilic microorganisms the sanitization of the mass, the abatement of the pathogen load and the inactivation of plant pests and weed seeds is achieved.

The composting process takes place at highly variable **pH** regimes; in the first stage, simple substances of an acidic nature, such as carbon dioxide or short-chain carboxylic acids, are produced; later due to aeration, the pH rises to values of 8 or 9, until it reaches neutrality at the end of the process.

The presence of **oxygen** is crucial to the process, as microorganisms require an aerobic environment to oxidize organic substances and derive energy from these oxidation-reduction reactions; should the oxygen content drop to values around 5 percent by volume anaerobic microorganisms would take over, resulting in the development of anaerobic processes and the inevitable production of toxic and foul-smelling substances *(mercaptans, phosphines, ammonia, etc.)*.

Total substrate **porosity** is a measure of the voids existing in the biomass being composted and is determined by calculating the ratio, expressed as a percentage, between the volume occupied by the voids within the biomass and the volume occupied by the biomass itself. Air diffuses into the voids in competition with water, and the availability of the voids is closely dependent on particle size, particle size distribution of the materials and the continuity of the interstices between the particles.

Water plays a key role in the survival of microorganisms as it is a food source, a medium for the dissolution of atmospheric oxygen and the diffusion of nutrients, and an important factor in the thermoregulation of the system. For these reasons, composting piles must be sufficiently moist to allow adequate microbial activity without, however, preventing oxygenation of the mass. Therefore, **moisture** values must be compatible with an aerobic condition *(optimal range of 50 to 55 percent).*

Microorganisms active in the composting process need carbon as an energy source and nitrogen to synthesize proteins. The **C/N ratio** is an index of control of microbial activity within the composting process. An excess of carbon causes a slowdown in microbial activity and thus decomposition, while an excess of nitrogen results in losses through ammonia volatilization, especially at high pH and temperature. At the end of the process a good quality product has C/N ratio values between 10 and 20. *But who are the real players in the composting process?*

Hot Composting Vs Cold Composting

We have seen how compost is decomposed organic matter. Compost can be obtained from garden waste, for example, which can consist of shredded branches, leaves and tops of perennials, and green kitchen scraps. Garden waste is turned into compost by a microbiological process in which microorganisms such as fungi decompose dead organic matter. The organic material we put in the compost bin, such as leaves and branch waste, is called *windrow*.

Fully decomposed compost is a dark brown residue that is relatively rich in potassium and phosphorus, but relatively poor in nitrogen. When compost comes into contact with the soil, it becomes what we call humus. The main advantage of storing as much garden waste as possible on your land is that you can get a good, nutrient-rich compost to spread on the garden soil to improve the soil. In particular, soil structure and microflora improve if you improve the soil with compost. There are two ways to compost: *cold composting and hot composting.*

When dead plant components fall to the ground, they decay. You can also put dead plant pieces in flower beds to decay in the landscape. Small branches and stems can also be cut into smaller pieces. Hedge cuttings can also be broken up and pushed under the hedge. Mulch maintains moisture in the soil and decomposes into compost, which improves the soil. You may keep your garden clean and neat by collecting garden debris in a compost bin or compost bin. Green kitchen leftovers can also be composted. This will increase the finished compost's nutrient content. At the same time, it enables you to use compost precisely where soil improvement is most needed in the garden.How to make cold compost

1) Put a layer of smaller branches and twigs in the bottom of the compost bin.

2) Mix garden and kitchen scraps well and put them on top.

3) You can keep adding new green waste until the bin is full. Remember to mix the different types of waste.

4) Water the heap well.

5) If necessary, cover the heap with a tarp to retain moisture and prevent nutrients from being washed away when it rains. Remember to water the heap if it is covered.

6) Decomposition is faster if you stir the compost from time to time, that is, mix the material or move it to a new pile.

7) After 1-2 years, the compost is completely transformed. The partially transformed compost can also be used as a ground cover.

How To Make Hot Compost

Hot composting requires large amounts of garden and kitchen waste and a little more effort, but it has more advantages than cold composting:

- Disease germs, pests and weeds are killed because the composted material reaches about 60°C (140°F) temperature during decomposition. Replacement is faster.
- After only 2-3 months you will have half the compost. After ½ year it is fully converted.

In order to make hot compost you need:

1) A large pile of garden waste, at least 1 cubic yard and preferably more. This is necessary to allow the temperature inside the heap to rise sufficiently during decomposition.

2) The pile should be covered with a tarp, an old blanket, a thick layer of straw or similar to keep the heat in.

3) If you want to be sure to kill disease germs and weeds, the heap should be staked after a few weeks, when the temperature inside the heap starts to drop. This means that the composting material should be moved with a handle so that the outside material goes inside and vice versa.

4) If you choose hot composting, you cannot use compost worms, which develop best at a temperature of about 25° C (77°F). Compost worms die if the temperature drops below freezing or exceeds 28°C (82°F).

Aerobic Vs. Anaerobic

Aerobic composting

Aerobic composting is the set of natural processes that lead to the degradation of the organic fraction of waste, thanks to the action of a series of microorganisms operating in oxygen-rich environments and leading to the production of a family of compounds known as humus(humic and fulvic acids). Three phases are usually distinguished in the aerobic process:

In the first (known as the mesophilic or latency phase) the growth of bacteria is observed, which initiate the degradation of carbohydrates, lipids and proteins, producing carbon dioxide and water, as well as causing a rapid rise in temperature.

In the next phase (called thermophilic or stabilization) temperatures exceed 120 degrees: in such an environment only thermophilic bacteria resist and bioxidative phenomena accelerate, during which ammonia is released and the death of pathogens results.

In the last stage (cooling or ripening), fungi and actinomycetes intervene and begin the degradation of cellulose and lignin with humus formation. Contextually, temperature and pH are lowered and microbial activity decreases.

Anaerobic Composting

The absence of oxygen is the feature that differentiates this process of biological decomposition of organic sewage of animal origin (also known as "anaerobic digestion") from aerobic composting. Bacteria naturally present in sewage, solid waste and, more generally, in any waste of organic origin, develop and multiply, feeding on the organic substances present.

As a consequence, there is a reduction in the mass of waste, as a result of the production of gaseous chemical compounds: biogas, a mixture consisting mainly of methane and carbon dioxide. In the anaerobic process, carbohydrates, proteins and lipids in the organic matter are broken down into simpler substances (fatty acids, monosaccharides, amino acids, alcohols) through the action of hydrolytic and fermentative bacteria (so-called hydrolysis). Then acidogenic bacteria use these products by transforming them into even simpler molecules, such as volatile fatty acids with production of ammonia, carbon dioxide, hydrogen sulfide (acidogenesis). The simple molecules produced are then further digested producing carbon dioxide, hydrogen, and acetic acid (acetogenesis).

Finally, these latter products are attacked by methanigenic and hydrogenotrophic bacteria and transformed into methane, carbon dioxide, and water.

Benign Bacteria, Microorganisms And Molds

The microorganisms naturally present in the organic matrix are the real architects of the composting process, and therefore knowledge of the different microbial groups involved and their role is extremely relevant. Composting is a dynamic process that evolves through sequential stages in which the process parameters change; this generates a consequent evolution in the microbial community that, at each stage, sees the prevalence of one or another microbial group. The microorganisms that operate in the composting process can be classified in relation to the temperature regimes in which they carry out their metabolic activity. Three classes are distinguished: *psychrophilic, mesophilic and thermophilic microorganisms.* There are three types of bacteria:

- Psychrophilic (low-temperature bacteria)
- Mesophilic (40-105°F / 5-40°C), which do most of the work in compost heaps.
- Thermophilic (105 – 200° F / 40-95°C)

In terms of numbers, bacteria represent the dominant part of the process agents, being about one hundred times higher than the other categories of microorganisms. They are typically associated with the consumption and degradation of readily biodegradable organic matter and are found throughout the mass. Bacteria are, in practice, the dominant population throughout the entire composting process, while fungi and actinomycetes generally proliferate in the more advanced stages of the process where there are generally conditions closer to mesophilicity and where competition with bacteria for readily biodegradable compounds is lessened in favor of lignin and waxes (which are more slowly biodegradable). In conclusion, we can say that the composting process performs, in our society, an important strategic and ecological-environmental function, because it transforms biomass from the urban waste collection cycle and from agricultural and agro-industrial activity into a real product useful for the fertilization of agricultural soils, no longer phytotoxic but a nutrient contributor and an improver of soil structural characteristics. Of note is the importance of the use of microorganisms also in the remediation of polluted soils, a technique better known as bioremediation.

WHAT TO COMPOST

In composting, we can bring in organic waste of all kinds. From kitchen waste, which includes vegetable peels and leftover food, to field and garden residues such as brushwood and grass clippings. Even paper and cardboard, if not treated with inks or plasticizers, are usable carbonaceous matter. All these can be added, always remembering the proper ratio of *"green matter"* to *"brown matter."* Here are all the helpful hints to avoid making those mistakes that could jeopardize the outcome of composting.

Green matter (N)

- Vegetable peels and scraps
- Grass clippings
- Leftover food scraps
- Pasta (raw or cooked)
- Stale bread
- Parts of green plants
- Citrus peel

Brown matter (C)

- Dried leaves
- Shredded twigs
- Nuts and shells (shredded)
- Wood sawdust (untreated)
- Paper
- Straw
- Coffee grounds

In addition, care must be taken to shred the tougher materials, such as walnut shells or twigs, which would otherwise take too long to degrade. For pruning residues, a bio-shredder allows them to be shredded into small pieces suitable for quick composting. This also avoids the polluting practice of burning brushwood. In the array of materials we can process, there are some that are important to pay special attention to.

Compostable Materials To Pay Attention To

Animal Waste
Meat and more generally animal waste, even cooked, could alter the process, since being very rich in nitrogen, they tend to be very putrescible. The result could be to attract animals to the surroundings (dogs, cats in general) and if these residues

unbalance the carbon-nitrogen ratio also to promote unpleasant smelling and unhealthy rots.

To remedy these problems, it is advisable to shred/grind and homogenize the material in question by increasing the amount of dry (carbonaceous) material. Those who are not very experienced are advised when in doubt not to compost animal residues, starting with vegetable composting. Over time you will learn better and gradually introduce small additions of animal waste.

Wood Ash

Another element that needs attention is wood ash. A very important element since it adds important minerals to the compost, and thus in the future to our soil. It should be used with gradual and controlled additions. The reason is that ash significantly affects PH, being very alkaline (raises PH, contains sodium hydroxide). So the advice is to use it in low dosages, approximately 1lb per cubic feet. In addition, if we have a lot of ash, we could also spread it directly in the field/garden/yard/yard, to the extent of 1oz per square yard, for a consistent supply to be practiced annually.

Citrus Peels

The peels of orange, lemon and other citrus fruits are somewhat slow to degrade, due to even natural waxy substances that create a film, plus they are an inherently acidic material. For this reason there is a widespread misconception that they should not be composted. In reality it is still organic matter that can be used in the compost bin or in heaps. The important thing is to chop up the peels, to speed up the process, and to adjust the dosage, avoiding excesses.

What not to compost

When making compost, it can happen that you make some mistakes and throw waste into the compost bin that could compromise the quality of the compost. To avoid making these mistakes, we will outline what not to put in the compost bin. Avoid all waste of synthetic origin, non-biodegradable or contaminated with toxic substances. Basically, they should not be thrown in the compost pile:

- Residues of diseased or infested plants: In fact, these should never be put in the compost heap; pathogens could survive composting and you could consequently transmit them to new crops using the compost in question.

- Lawn mowing, tree pruning and the vegetable garden, treated with pesticides: The wisest thing would be not to use pesticides for garden or lawn care, in any case be aware that synthetic products do not degrade during composting.

- Very aggressive weed parts: During the thermogenic phase, the increased temperature should deactivate the weed seeds making the compost pile weed-proof... However, this is only true in theory. In addition, remember that a new plant can grow from every weed root fragment!

- All the weeds that have gone to seed: As stated above, composting may not be able to neutralize those weed seeds, which, at a later time, you may find them just about everywhere in your garden when you go to use compost as fertilizer.

- Dog and cat litter: They could trigger a range of diseases.
- Leftover wood that has been painted or treated with chemicals.
- Leftover coated paper, i.e., from magazines.
- Textiles, plastics (even if biodegradable), expired medications, and of course anything that is not biodegradable.

COMPOSTING METHODS

Because everyone has various demands, one or more of these strategies may be appropriate for your current living conditions at any given time, and you may change your ways multiple times throughout your life. What was once useful may become obsolete as your requirements and environment change, thus it is important to understand the advantages and disadvantages of any system. What is a benefit to you may be a disadvantage to someone else. All you have to do is figure out what works best for you. They all serve diverse objectives to varying degrees, some more efficiently than others, and some are simply different. Perhaps you've tried some of these techniques before, are happy with your method, are searching for something to round out your system, or want to change. I hope this information sheds light on aspects you may not have considered when selecting your previous composter or when purchasing a new composter.

Trench Composting

Trench composting is a method of composting kitchen and garden waste, such as weeds, that requires little effort on your side and improves soil health in just one month. This composting method may be utilized anyplace in your garden and cannot be seen or smelled. What is the most enjoyable aspect? It is not necessary to turn it. Composting in a trench is a straightforward procedure. In an empty place in the garden, you dig a 12-inch-deep trench or hole of any form. Then you fill it with four to six inches of biodegradable materials such as kitchen garbage, dead garden plants, tiny prunings, weeds, or thinnings and cover it with the earth from the trench or hole. *The next step... well there isn't one!*

Benefits of trench composting

The ease of trench composting is the best incentive to do it. There is no need to worry about keeping an appropriate moisture level, aerating, or sifting as there is with a compost heap. Other reasons to experiment with trench composting include:

- Trench composting delivers nutrients to plants exactly where they are needed: in the root zone. Plant roots delve deep into the earth in quest of the nourishment that you have buried. As a result, neighboring plants benefit in two ways: They are fed by organic particles in the excavation and have a strong and deep root system. The plants can withstand drought and heat better and require less attention from the grower.

- Compost has no odor and is invisible. Many people are concerned about where to put the compost heap. Although there are numerous ways for composting in tiny spaces, trench composting entirely solves this issue because the trash is buried wherever there is an open place in the yard. Even the stinkiest kitchen garbage will not be a problem because it will be buried under several inches of soil.

- Even though it is not permitted, it is a method of composting. Home composting is prohibited in several municipalities and city complexes. This is an excellent covert method.

Disadvantages of trench composting

Although trench composting has many advantages, there are also potential drawbacks to consider.

- Regular maintenance is required for trench composting since it is vital to keep adding material to the trench and turning it on a regular basis.

- Might attract animals: Composting in trenches can attract animals who are drawn to food waste.

- Time-consuming: It can take a long time to dig the trench, load it with organic debris, and then cover it.

- Causes unpleasant odors: Another potential disadvantage of trench composting is that it can cause unpleasant odors if done incorrectly. This is frequently caused by adding too much food waste to the trench or using insufficient organic stuff to cover it.

Equipment required
- Garden shovel
- Bucket
- Lots of cranking power

Start-up & maintenance procedure:

1) Locate a good area; preferably one that is easily accessible from where you will create the biodegradable material (typically from your kitchen) and where you want the soil to be enriched (such as a garden or a future vegetable garden).

2) Make a hole big enough to fit the biodegradable material in. The depth of the hole should be between 4 and 8 in, so that at least 6 in of dirt ends up on top of the stuff. It is quite effective to dig ahead of time and create a long trench.

3) Set away scattered earth: Be careful not to scatter the earth while you dig. Make a pile of it to cover the compost afterwards.

4) Keep scraps or garden trash: If you haven't already, save vegetable peelings and other food waste to use as filler in the hole. You'll get a lot of advise on what you should and cannot compost, but we threw virtually everything in there. According to my knowledge, using the feces of animals capable of eating meat is risky (so not even those of vegetarian dogs). I've heard of people putting toilet paper or used Kleenex in there. I would also avoid using newspapers and other printed materials; once again, consider what the content includes and make your own decisions.

5) Cover the biodegradable material with reserved dirt: You can apply dirt to the biodegradable material as you go or all at once. A shovel should be kept near the trench.

6) Allow microorganisms, worms, and insects to perform their jobs! You should have lovely soil in less than a year, depending on the type of soil, the amount of water, and the temperature. When we dig, I plant small seed flowers or a 'green manure' crop on it the first year, and then we till it the next spring.

Pile Composting

Organic debris is heaped up in pile composting and then degraded by bacteria. As the heap decomposes, nutrients and heat are released back into the compost. The quantity of heat in the heap determines whether it is hot or cold:

The hot heap *(with temperatures ranging from 113°F to 160°F)* promotes rapid decomposition and is devoid of weed seeds, diseases, and insect eggs, which can survive for many days at temperatures as high as 135°F. Hot heaps require more upkeep than cold heaps because they must maintain a continual high temperature. Adequate ventilation and humidity levels are critical for maintaining microbial activity, regulating temperature, and ensuring heat is delivered uniformly throughout the pile.

The cold heap temperatures *(reaching 70°F and 90°F)* are affected by the surrounding ambient air, resulting in a significantly lower total temperature and a lot slower decomposition. Weeds and anything that can spread bugs or pathogens should not be added to a cold heap since the temperatures required to kill them are not reached. Because there is no need to maintain a continuous temperature range, cold composting requires less upkeep. Simply pile the greens and browns together and turn them from time to time.

Benefits of pile composting

- It's simple: rotting food does the dirty work for you.

- Reduced waste: Consider the waste reduction in your kitchen while composting to get a sense of how a composting nation can minimize waste in city dumps.

- The kitchen smells nicer now: The scent of decomposition from the garbage bin will not enter the kitchen if fruit and vegetable peels end up in the compost bin.

- It is inexpensive: There is no need for technical equipment if you opt to produce a compost pile; you may build your own bin or buy one for a low cost.

- It has the potential to save you money: You will pay less rubbish to transport if you have to pay the refuse service for each bag. Even if you do not pay for the bag, if a large number of individuals in your neighborhood begin composting, the city's garbage expenditures will be reduced. Residents will benefit from these savings in the form of lower property taxes.

- Rich fertilizer is produced: Composting trash decomposes quickly into a nutrient-rich organic fertilizer that may be sieved and utilized to benefit the garden, landscape, and grass. This fertilizer also has an economic benefit in that it eliminates the need to buy fertilizer at the garden center; compost-fed gardens also use less water and fertilizer to achieve the same amount of growth as a garden with no decomposed matter in the soil.

Disadvantages of pile composting

- Pile composting produces odors and takes up space: composting should not smell terrible if the dry to wet composting material ratio is correct and no ingredients such as meat have been added. However, especially in hot summer temperatures, it can still smell like decomposing material. There is also enough for a composting facility.

- Infections can be spread by unhealthy plants: If you remove sick or diseased plants from the vegetable garden, you cannot put them in the compost heap without potentially spreading pathogens passed from the soil to the plants seasoned with the compost. You should also avoid putting ripped weeds in the compost heap to keep them from reproducing.

- Although the work connected with pile composting is minimal, it does take time and effort to get started and separate the materials appropriate for composting from the food waste.

Equipment required

- Compost bin
- Shovel

- Bucket
- Pitchfork

Start-up & maintenance procedure

The simplest way to compost is to make a pile or heap in the garden and tend to it as needed. Put it somewhere dry and shady, preferably near a water supply.

- Make a clearing in your yard or garden to expose bare soil.
- Make a straw or twig foundation layer. A few inches will help with drainage.
- Layer composting elements on top of one another, alternating brown and green materials.
- To begin decomposition, add a nitrogen source. To begin the process, some gardeners apply a handful of nitrogen fertilizer.
- Maintain the heap's moisture. It is suggested that the materials be wet enough to feel the water but not so wet that you can squeeze it out if you take a handful.
- Turn the compost heap every two weeks to allow the center to 'warm up.' Aeration both oxygenates the microorganisms engaged in composting and mixes the heap.

Tumbler Composting

Compost Tumblers will save you from one of the most time-consuming aspects of composting: 'turning' the compost heap. This operation is typically accomplished with a pitchfork in open composters where there is enough area to wield a tool. Turning the pile speeds up the composting process by aerating and mixing the heated composting material with freshly added materials, hence bringing microbial activity that aids in the breakdown of new materials. As a consequence, you'll have a rich, ready-to-use compost.

Composters are completely sealed containers that can be rotated to mix the composting contents. The sealed container also helps to keep the heat generated by the composting process contained, which speeds up the process of transforming kitchen and garden waste into compost. Compost containers were created to make composting easier and more efficient. Compost bins and drum composters are not the same thing.

Composters are intended to be placed on the ground, and the majority have an open bottom. Although compost bins are the least expensive type of composter, they have several drawbacks: it is difficult to turn the compost with a pitchfork, heat readily dissipates, slowing the composting process, and mice can easily dig under the sides to obtain the composting ingredients.

Benefits of tumbler composting:
- **It hastens the composting process:** in a sealed compost tumbler, waste can be converted into finished household

compost in as little as three weeks under optimal conditions. The ambient temperature, the time of year, and the proper balance of carbon and nitrogen are all elements that influence composting pace. In colder and wetter climates, the composting process will take much longer than three weeks.

- **Protects the compost from mice, raccoons, and other animals:** Compost tumblers are often elevated above the ground and composed of durable, animal-resistant materials.

- **Composting odors are eliminated:** The compost tumbler' closed design prevents odors from escaping.

- **Neat and appealing:** Compost bins are suited for urban and suburban residential homes due to their attractive design and clean operation.

Disadvantages of tumbler composting:

- **Usually more costly than composters:** compost tumblers are often constructed of sturdier materials to accommodate moist and heavy composting ingredients. This is not an issue with drum-type composters because the baskets are open-bottomed and do not need to support any weight. Basket composters also have support legs or bottoms with rollers, which makes them more expensive to manufacture.

- **Units with capacities greater than 9.5 feet may be difficult to turn:** most drum-style composters have capacity of 9.5 cubic feet or less. This is due to the fact that a larger drum is more difficult to turn when full. However, higher capacity rotating composters with a mechanical aid (such as a rod and gear system) are available. Smaller types are easier to turn.

Equipment required

- Compost Tumbler
- Shovel
- Bucket

Start-up & maintenance procedure

If you have the correct equipment and techniques, starting a compost tumbler is simple and convenient. In this part, we will go over the procedures for starting a compost tumbler. Follow the instructions below:

1) **Determine the best place:** The location you pick is critical, because composting works best in areas with enough humidity and sunlight to boost temperature. Placing tumblers in direct sunlight can cause the procedure to take longer. You can store your composter beneath a tree. If you don't have a tree, place it on the west or south side of your house.

2) **Gather green trash:** Compost heaps are made up of two primary parts. The first is nitrogen-rich garbage, sometimes known as green waste. These organic materials are high in nitrogen and other nutrients like phosphorus and potassium. When you finish composting, all of the nutrients in the compost are derived primarily

from green waste. This means that nutrient-rich green waste must be sought out and included in the compost heap. You can shred green trash into tiny pieces to assist composting bacteria break it down more efficiently. Other sorts of garbage should also be collected in the compost heap to speed up the composting process.

3) **Gather brown trash:** In contrast to green waste, the primary goal of brown garbage is not to enrich compost. Instead, it serves to boost the energy level of the compost heap's decomposing bacteria. Brown waste has a higher carbon content than other nutrients. Composting bacteria use carbon-rich waste as sugar (carbohydrates). Composting bacteria require energy to decompose your compost heap, just as you do to digest food. Microbes get their energy from brown trash. Other benefits of brown trash include:

- Many varieties of brown waste are dry and absorb a significant amount of moisture: Although moisture is necessary for composting, too much of it might cause fermentation (which occurs in an oxygen-depleted environment) rather than decomposition (for aerobic organisms such as fungi).

- Avoids odors: keep in mind that green waste is high in nitrogen. The majority of nitrogen-rich organic waste, such as animal manure, includes nitrogen in the form of ammonia. The compost heap will smell of ammonia if there is too much green trash. Brown garbage, like green waste, must be shredded before being added to the compost heap.

4) **Add garbage to the compost tumbler:** When you've gathered enough trash, toss it into the compost heap. Check that you have enough waste. Depending on the humidity in your location, you should add garbage in a ratio of one part green waste to two or three parts brown waste. Add less brown trash if you reside in a dry environment (low humidity).

5) **(OPTIONAL) Fill the tumbler with a starter or compost accelerator:** The compost barrel rests on top of the soil, which is a slight disadvantage of composting with the tumbler. Although this can be beneficial, relocating the barrel further from the soil can limit bacteria such as fungi's access to the compost bin. The compost heap may not decompose if these bacteria are not there.

6) It is recommended that a compost starter be added to the tumbler to aid in the decomposition of the compost heap. These products introduce beneficial bacteria that breakdown the heap quickly. It is critical to place this product in the tumbler composter.

7) **Turn the compost tumbler on a regular basis:** The majority of composter manufacturers recommend turning or rotating the composter at least once each day. Some, on the other hand, recommend flipping it every other day. You must follow the manufacturer's directions for your composter. Keep in mind that turning the compost heap is vital to ensure that the trash decomposes swiftly. Check that the composter has holes

that allow oxygen, carbon dioxide, and other gases to pass through.

8) **Water the compost heap on a regular basis:** Never let the compost pile dry out. Depending on the humidity in your area, you can water the heap once or twice a week. Use clean water and avoid overwatering the heap to the point where it drips. If the mound leaks, gather the water and use it to irrigate your crops because it's high in nutrients.

9) **Keep track of the compost:** After placing the compost heap in the composter and stirring it on a regular basis, you should examine the compost heap for the following:

    - The temperature of the compost heap does not require the use of a thermometer. You should be able to feel the heat radiated by the heap if you open the container. If the heap does not emit heat, it is not composting.

    - Smell: A typical compost heap should have an earthy or similar odor to the waste that is deposited in it. If the odor is strong, such as ammonia or rotten eggs, extra brown waste should be added.

    - Pests: Examine the pile for centipedes, centipedes, lizards, and other pests that can enter the barrel openings. These bugs must be removed because they can contaminate the waste heap by landing on it (altering the ratio of green to brown waste).

    - If your heap is in good condition, the waste should decompose quickly.

10) **Determine whether the compost is ready:** Most compost piles should be finished in less than two months. Although compost heap makers claim that the heap can be finished in a fortnight, this is not guaranteed. When the heap is finished, it will have an earthy odor (uniform aroma), an even consistency, and will be slightly dark brown.

Worm Composting

Worm composting (sometimes spelled vermicomposting) is a major boon. It provides an easy way to dispose of organic waste like vegetable peelings. It helps the environment by saving space in county landfills. Worms find a pleasant home and plenty of free 'meal.' Home-grown compost is an excellent technique to nourish and nurture plants in gardens or container plants. Vermiculture, which some proponents refer to as "organic waste disposal," converts food waste into a rich, dark, and beneficial soil conditioner for your plants. Worm composting, contrary to popular belief, does not have to be a stinky operation. Your compost bin should not smell if you take adequate care of it.

Benefits of worm composting
- **Speed:** worm composting produces ready-to-use manure in 2-3 months, whilst other composting processes require 6-9 months.
- **The setting:** worm composting can be done both inside and outside. Composting bins can even be installed

beneath the kitchen sink. This is one of the most significant advantages it has over other composting methods. Simply break the organic stuff into little pieces so that the worms can eat it fast and the system remains odor-free.

- **Extra worms:** At the end of the composting cycle, you'll have more worms than you did at the start. Once every 90 days, these worms reproduce and treble their population. You may either put the extra worms to your garden to replenish the soil or feed them to your animals.
- **E. coli count:** According to recent research, vermicomposting reduces the amount of E. coli bacteria to acceptable levels after 21 days.
- **Decentralization:** Because it is easily implemented in rural and urban houses, it eliminates transporting organic waste to centralized areas. This, in turn, saves fuel for transportation, lowering community expenditures and CO_2 emissions.

Disadvantages of worm composting

- **Pathogens:** Because there is no heat build-up, pathogens are not eliminated as quickly in vermicomposting as they are in traditional composting.
- **Cost:** Because containers and worms must be purchased, the initial cost of a vermicomposting system might be considerable.
- **Fruit flies:** Once loaded with organic debris, the containers might attract fruit flies. However, this

problem can be addressed by supplying food in sufficient quantities for the worms to consume and covering it with compost.

Equipment required

- A plastic container with a lid
- Drilling and drilling bits
- A plastic container or bowl (for soaking newspaper, cardboard, etc.)
- Cardboard and newspaper (for bedding)
- Water (normal city water or tap water is fine)
- Compost (enough to fill the bottom of a 2"-3" bin)
- 1-2 pound red worms

Start up & maintenance

As a seasoned gardener, I've tried nearly every organic fertilizer on the market. Although all have produced positive effects, worm composting, worm castings, and 'worm tea' have particularly impressed me. Worm composting has the major advantage of being able to be done at home, allowing for year-round composting. Vermicompost is a good organic fertilizer and nutrient-rich soil conditioner because it includes nutrients and water-soluble bacteria. Each day, one libbre of red worms can consume one to half a libbre of garbage. They convert the trash into organic humus, which is high in nutrients and helpful bacteria.

Worms: One of the most widespread misconceptions among beginners in vermicomposting is that any earthworm can be used for worm composting (or kept at home, for that matter). This is not entirely correct. The worms found in the garden and yard are anecic in nature. They are dirt worms that like to have their own place. Composting worms are of the 'epigeal' variety. They prefer to live in rich organic material (rather than soil) and are accustomed to being surrounded by their peers. Eisenia fetida, popularly known as the red worm or red wiggler, is the most prevalent type of composting worm.

Configuration of containers: There is no 'wrong' size for a worm bin; nonetheless, the surface area must be prioritized. A larger surface area provides for more oxygenation of the container and allows the worms to better spread themselves. As a result, a tank is far superior to a bucket. Because red worms (and earthworms in general) are extremely sensitive to direct light, the container must be opaque, rather than transparent, and have a lid to keep light out. A container with an easily removable lid is preferred.

Environment: It is estimated that half a kilogram of worms are used per square metre of surface area. The container utilized in this piece was approximately 20 square feet in size. Compost worms require food as well as a living environment. Both are provided by the 'bedding' material we shall utilize. To keep appropriate moisture, the optimum living environment comprises plenty of bedding material, waste material, and water. Worms enjoy a dark, cool environment with temperatures ranging from 40 to 80 degrees. Let us proceed to the construction of our container without further ado. The following items will be required:

Procedure:

1) Using the drill, drill 1/8"-1/4" holes every 2-3 inches in the lid for air and ventilation. Then, along the top of the container, drill a row (or two) of holes. You may have read that you must drill holes in the bottom of the bin to collect the 'leachate' (liquid from the jets) and that you must have a tray or second bin to collect it. This, in my opinion, is not essential. If you soak the bedding material properly, the inside bottom of the bin does not become overly saturated and does not 'bog down.' You can line the inside bottom of the container with one or two layers of cardboard if you choose.

2) Fill the bin with about 2 inches of compost and level it. This serves as a home and workplace for the worms. If you bought worms locally or online, they may have already been packed around some compost. You can surely utilize that compost and mix it with the prepared compost in such instance.

3) It's worm time. Insert the worms into the compost base. They will vanish virtually instantly in the compost and out of sight.

4) It's littering time. Fill the second bin or container halfway with water. Take the newspaper and tear it into one-inches-wide strips. The newspaper has a 'grain,' and it tends to shred more easily along the grain. The grain of the newspaper I chose runs vertically from top to bottom. Shredded cardboard and autumn leaves are two other types of bedding to consider. Simply shred cardboard and cut up leaves into small pieces.

5) Dip the newspaper into the water for a few seconds and soak it. The moisture content of the worm bedding should be comparable to a wrung-out sponge. Place the newspaper in the container after squeezing it until most of the water has drained off. Because it will be a solid, moist ball, separate the parts as much as you can.

6) Repeat STEP 5 until you have a 6-8 inch layer of damp bedding. I filled the container until the holes drilled in the container's sides were completely covered. I sprayed the topmost newspaper strips with water rather than soaking them. At this stage, the container is nearly complete. It is not required to feed the worms at this time. I was informed that one should wait a week for the worms to settle before adding food trash for them to eat on. In terms of eating, below is a general list of what is and is not recommended:

Reccomended:

- Fruit and vegetable waste (citrus fruits should be used sparingly). Pineapple and mango should be absolutely avoided).
- Starchy foods such as bread, pasta, rice, and potatoes are acceptable in moderation.
- Newspaper shreds and cardboard
- Ground egg shells - in moderation
- Coffee grounds/filters - use sparingly.
- Tissues

Not recommended:

- Human or animal waste
- Non-biodegradable materials
- Meat or dairy products
- Any chemical compounds
- Oils or fats

Bin Composting

By providing proper air and moisture retention, most compost containers are designed to speed the breakdown of organic matter. The right balance of air and moisture offers ideal conditions for the aerobic organisms that generate the high temperatures that convert organic materials into compost. Even without a structure to hold the waste, decomposition will occur over time in a 'pile' or 'heap' of compost. Having a compost bin, on the other hand, is advantageous since it speeds up decomposition and keeps the environment clean. Some bins are continuous, which means you may continue to add trash, whilst others generate compost batches with a predefined combination of elements that must be added all at once. Bins can also make it more difficult for mice to obtain the compost, depending on the design. This is especially true of the basket kind. Let's have a look at the benefits and drawbacks of bin composting.

Benefits of bin composting:

- Lowest composter price
- A lot of volume in a limited space
- More easily removes extra moisture

Disadvantages of bin composting:

- Thinner plastic that can crack or be broken by tools
- It is difficult to obtain completed compost.
- Can entice and harbor pests like mice

Start up & maintenance:

1) **Choosing biological matter for the composter:** a properly operating composter needs both carbon-rich (brown) and nitrogen-rich (green) components. Microorganisms need carbon and nitrogen to feed and strengthen themselves in order to generate compost.

2) **Gather organic materials for your compost heap:** gather enough brown and green materials to construct a compost heap at least one metre high before you begin. This magnitude will enhance the possibility of failure. Greens may be stored in closed tubs, while browns can be stored in buckets until you run out. Collect at least twice the number of browns as greens.

3) **Adding organic materials to the compost bin in strategic layers:** once you have a good collection of

greens and browns, place them in the compost bin. Begin by applying a 2 in thick coat of browns. Lightly wet the layer. Then add a layer of veggies about 2 in high. This layer should also be lightly watered. Continue alternating brown and green layers, culminating with a brown covering to keep flies out and scents in. Browns should outnumber greens in the pile because they let air and water to circulate, keeping microorganisms healthy and happy. A stinking compost heap indicates that you require more browns. If the pile does not begin to heat up, you will almost certainly need more green.

4) **Adjust the compost heap's moisture level:** it's time to start digging! Squeeze some compost from your mound. If the moisture content is comparable to that of a wrung-out sponge, it is correct (damp but not soggy). If the heap is too dry, add more water; if it is too wet, add more brown.

5) **Circulate the air in the compost heap:** turn the heap on a frequent basis to keep it aerated and decomposing effectively. Turn the mound with a garden fork or spade often at first (every one or two days), then once or twice a week. Look for signs that your compost is ready to use: if you carefully care for your compost heap, you should be able to have a fresh batch of compost in three to six months. It is ready when the color is black and rich, the consistency is crumbly and silky, and the aroma is earthy and woody.

Bokashi Composting

The Japanese term for *"organic matter that has been fermented"* is "bokashi," which translates to "fermented organic material." Dr. Teuro Higa, a professor at Ryukyus University in Okinawa, Japan, created the approach in the early 1980s. To do so, you must use a designated bucket and a Bokashi inoculant to combine food scraps (fruit and vegetable peels, egg shells, and meat and dairy scraps). Most inoculants contain a mixture of wheat germ, wheat bran, or sawdust, molasses, and live bacteria (EM). These microorganisms, which are identical to those found in soil, get their sustenance from the bran and molasses. You may find Bokashi composting components, such as active bacteria and bran/molasses, and whole Bokashi composting kits online, at garden stores, and at natural product retailers. On the other hand, you may create your own setup.

Bokashi buckets have a lid that seals tightly and a tap at the bottom that allows liquid to be drained. A foul odor can be avoided by draining the liquid, but the resulting "bokashi tea" can be used to nourish houseplants. After being piled and shielded from the sun, the mixture quickly ferments and can be dug into the garden or added to a standard compost bin or heap to disintegrate in about ten days. In any case, action can begin right away. The Bokashi method differs from the conventional composting strategy in that it relies more on fermentation than on mechanical decomposition.

Bokashi is an anaerobic procedure, meaning that as much oxygen as possible must be removed from the ingredients before the process can begin. Aerobic conditions are ideal for the composting process used traditionally. The garbage container should only be opened when trash is being added to prevent contamination. Some individuals suggest covering rubbish that will be composted with a flat surface, such as a plate, to keep it from being exposed to oxygen while it sits in the composter. Since bokashi composting is an anaerobic process that ferments rather than fully digests biological components, it differs from other composting methods. That's what separates it from other composting methods. When compared to conventional composting methods, Bokashi composting produces leftovers that are both very nutrient-dense for plants and useful as "fuel" for other composting methods. Despite the fact that unique tools and supplies are needed for this kind of composting, it is becoming increasingly popular.

GOOD TO KNOW: Another significant factor to consider is that this smart Japanese method is ideal for tiny indoor areas. This approach is for you if you live in an apartment and can't (or don't want to) run up and down stairs to get to the compost.

Advantages of bokashi composting

- The method makes use of milk and meat waste that would otherwise go to waste in other types of composting.
- Bokashi composting may be done in a small space since the components do not need to be inflated with air.
- The finished product is a very nourishing plant food that may be buried in garden composting trenches.

- The liquid by-product makes an excellent fertilizer tea that can be applied straight to plants.
- The fermented material is ideal for feeding worm composting containers.

<u>Disadvantages of bokashi composting</u>
- Unlike conventional compost, which may be used as mulch in the garden above ground, the material created is fermented. To decompose further, it must be buried in garden trenches or added to a typical compost heap.
- The technique requires the use of a certain airtight bucket or container that can drain the liquid generated.

<u>Start up & maintenance</u>
1) To begin the bokashi process, sprinkle a thin coating of dusting to the bucket's bottom.
2) Fill the bucket with food waste once or twice a day, taking care not to open it too much to stymie the bokashi process. You can add any type of food except liquids and oils.
3) Add in 1-2 teaspoons bokashi for every 2 in layer of food
4) Crush the food as you go to let the air out. For this stage, use a potato masher. After using the bucket, carefully close the lid.
5) A liquid may collect at the bottom of the container as the kitchen waste ferments. Every 2-3 days, this liquid must be drained. When used undiluted, this liquid can be used

to clean toilets, sinks, and other drains. The liquid is an excellent garden fertilizer when diluted 1:100 with water, or 2-3 tablespoons per 2 gallons.

6) When the bucket is filled, close the cover and store it somewhere warm but not in direct sunshine.

7) Allow it to ferment for 10-14 days. Remember to drain the liquid every 2-3 days. The food residue should smell like pickles, and a white mould should form on top, indicating that the system is working properly.

Composting Machine

A composting machine for organic waste is used to recycle various forms of garbage and turn it into compost that may be used in a variety of ways. These devices make organic waste disposal easier; without them, the same process would take a long period. The overall procedure deals with garbage mounds that pollute the environment. The organic waste composting machine is designed to accelerate the composting process and recycle as much garbage as possible in the shortest amount of time. The garbage composting machine operates on a straightforward concept. To begin, raw material is combined with water to make a mixture that can be utilized as input. From the input part, the waste is subsequently fed into the machine. The device has a mechanism for adding microorganisms to the mixture. Some holes provide air to the mixture. The trash mixture is mixed with the microorganisms using an agitating shaft. The temperature within the machine climbs to 120-150 degrees fahrenheit during the next seven days, eliminating undesired microorganisms and converting trash into safe and beneficial compost. When the composting process is finished, the temperature change stops, and organic fertilizers can be collected from the waste part.

All of this is now possible because to technological advancements. For example, modern composting devices can compost garbage in a single day. These machines use mixers and shredders to help break down garbage faster. Furthermore, some machines use PLC control systems and solar dewatering systems to speed up the composting process. Aside from rapid conversion, the devices differ in waste management. An organic composting machine is a cutting-edge and cost-effective waste management solution. The majority of garbage, particularly edible waste, can be recycled into something valuable. To begin with, employing a composting machine saves time and work in the process of converting trash into fertilizer. These organic fertilizers are pure and can be used to create healthy crops. It also eliminates the need for waste handling and transportation, which is important in a waste-filled environment. The environmental benefits are substantial.

Organic fertilizers improve the soil in addition to reducing methane emissions. Organic fertilizers provide nutrients to the soil that can be used in plantations. Compost, when added to the soil, reduces soil erosion and water retention. A full solution for a greener, more sustainable future is an organic waste machine. The organic waste composting machine is a useful technology that is utilized in a variety of industries, including hospitality, education, and food. Composting devices that are faster and more advanced are appearing on the market as technology progresses.

Advantages of composting machines:

- **It is quick in processing:** processing times for organic waste composting using machine technology are shorter than those using manual labor alone. Composting organic waste can free up resources for use in other areas of production.

- **It is completely automated:** with no human interaction required, the machine is efficient. It is possible for one person to handle it on their own, usually in their spare time.

- **Pathogens are eliminated:** composting machinery is used to sterilize organic waste. Compost has a longer shelf life and less chance of attracting pests after being pasteurized.

- **It has cheap operating expenses:** Rent, inventory, insurance, R&D, and salary costs for a composting machine are budget-friendly.

- **Takes up little space:** the machine is more space-efficient than traditional composting methods because of the high efficiency of its mechanical treatment equipment, which is relatively small in size.

- **Can compost all organic waste types:** the machine can process virtually any type of organic waste into nutrient-rich composted manure. Composting is a common practice, and many different types of food, including vegetables and non-vegetables, eggs, fish, crabs, small bones, fruit and vegetable peels, and leftovers, are often added to the pile.

- **Aids in sterilization:** when compost is sterilized, all of the dangerous microorganisms and other kinds of life that might be lurking in there are killed out or rendered harmless. There will be less people getting sick from using the compost if this is done.

- **It is free of secondary pollution:** the machine method does not result in any byproducts. It doesn't smell bad and it won't hurt you.

- **It is long-lasting:** Machines are often constructed with a stainless steel tank with a lifespan of more than 20 years.

- **It can be purchased or rented:** Those in need of an organic waste composting machine have several options for obtaining one. They have the option of acquiring, renting, or leasing.

- **Has an efficient power control system:** The organic waste composting machine has power mode, heating mode, and power saving mode indications.

- **It decreases the need for additional methods of environmental waste treatment:** the technology inside the machine can compost food scraps in a landfill or incinerator-free environment.

- **Increases safety:** The overload feature prevents the machine from spilling waste or endangering the user when it becomes overloaded.

- **When the compost removal door is opened, the internal mixing blades come to a halt:** the composting machine is safer to operate thanks to this automatic action control system. Further, it simplifies the way of operation. The organic waste composting machine was a major advancement in the quest for reliable and environmentally friendly waste disposal methods. More and more people and businesses, both public and private, are realizing the advantages of these tools and purchasing them to recycle and transform their trash. Numerous consumers have taken an interest in composting machine technology due to its various benefits. The gadgets can compost waste indefinitely, are noiseless, don't release odors, and are mouse- and insect-free. As a rule of thumb, they can cut down on volume by between 80% and 90%.

Disadvantages of composting machines

- **Decomposition is incomplete:** One disadvantage of this system is the requirement for more composting of the trash, which does not completely disintegrate, necessitating the collection of the residual contents for further composting in a garden bed or bay composting system.

- **The issue of needing more room:** Composted waste must be removed and stored on a regular basis for collection. Additional storage space is required because a well-ventilated outside area or a room with an exhaust fan is required.

- **High initial and ongoing costs:** Because the machines require power to work, the purchase and maintenance expenses of both residential and commercial mechanical composting systems are substantial.

- **Cleaning Difficulties:** The equipment for both residential and commercial mechanical composting systems are tough to clean and maintain.

- **Additional pieces are required:** EMO is required for some mechanical composters. Furthermore, commercial and residential systems emit an earthy stench. However, it is critical to fully grasp the benefits and drawbacks of mechanical composting and other composting methods, especially if you have identified the best, most beneficial, and most appropriate way for your needs and those of your surroundings. All of these strategies serve various aims and so function to varying degrees. Although one of these ways may be more efficient than others, you may wish to try some of them, either to augment your current system or to fully replace it.

Start up & maintenance

- Drain as much water as possible from the food waste and remove any hard elements such as bones, shells, and so on.

- Open the compost bin lid and place the food trash inside.

- The food waste is automatically mixed with germs and air by the mixing blade.

- The microbe will continue to compost indefinitely.

- Normally, food waste decomposes in 24 hours.

- Allow the by-product to accumulate in the bin until it reaches the fill mark on the side of the bin before removing the compost for use (it usually takes a little over a month).

- You can now open the bin and remove some of the compost (it is always advisable to leave some to keep microorganisms and continue to add food waste as needed), and voila—you can apply your compost mixture to your plants to provide them with all of the nutrients they require to flourish.

COMPOST GATHERING AND USAGE

To enrich the soil of an organic vegetable garden, it is very important to contribute organic matter. Undoubtedly the cheapest and most environmentally friendly way to do this is to employ well-matured self-produced compost. The organic matter we provide with compost is invaluable in fine-tuning the soil; in addition to nourishing plants, it nourishes soil microorganisms and helps make the soil softer to work with and more capable of retaining moisture. It can be used in direct contact with roots and seeds: it is suitable as potting soil for potted plants, reseeding and thickening lawns. It should be mentioned that the nutrients in compost vary in relation to the waste used to produce it. After looking at how to produce the precious compost, the chemistry behind it and the different ways to brew it, let's see how best to employ it in various growing contexts, whether potted, garden or vegetable garden plants.

How To Tell If Compost Is Mature

Well-managed composting does not take long: with the right conditions in three to four months the process is complete. Of course, if we have been composting at home, continuing to add material, we have to count the months from the last input for everything to be processed. This is why it is useful to consider using two compost bins when managing organic waste. A good compost can be recognized by its appearance: it presents itself as a fairly uniform loam, has no smell but rather an undergrowth odour. If necessary, we can sift the material before using it. We take into account when calculating the timing that a cold winter or dry summer period can slow down the process. If we are not sure of the result, we can wait a few more months and use the compost after 6-9 months.

TIP: If you want to check if your compost is really mature, do the watercress test. For this you need three small flower pots, two of them filled with compost and one filled with absorbent cotton or similar material. Sow the watercress. If, after seven days, as many cress plants have developed in the compost pots as in the cotton pot, the compost is mature.

How To Use Compost

Compost is perfectly fine for plants grown in pots, as long as it is well mature and has completely stopped decomposition so as to ward off the formation of mold that can seriously compromise the root system of plants: to be really sure that this does not happen, it is best to use compost that is at least a year and a half old. In principle, the best mix is achieved by combining 40-50% compost with 40-50% peat and the remainder sand. These doses usually cover the needs of the vast majority of cultivable plants; a slightly different matter when it comes to the cultivation of acidophilic plants for which the percentage of peat must go up to 60-70%.

Also with regard to its use in the garden, compost must be fully processed and mature and must have spent a minimum of one year inside the compost bin or heap. Its use is valuable both for improving soil structure, fertilizing the soil, and as an organic reserve for plants. Like manure, compost is able to improve overly compacted soils by spreading it on the surface and burying it later: this operation is well done during the fall or winter, that is, when normal tillage is carried out using preferably a lightly screened compost. The recommended amount is around 2-3 quintals per hundred square yard or, if you prefer, 1lb per square yard.

This amount can increase to 2-6 lb/sq yd if you intend to improve the fertility of poor soils; in this case compost can also be used fresher, trying to bury it deeper.

Its use as a nutrient in the garden is manifold and versatile: it ranges from spreading it around trees, adding it to flower beds, covering bulbs, at the foot of roses and hedges, etc. In short, we can indulge ourselves with its use as long as we do so, always using it with some caution and preferring low dosages, if anything to be repeated if necessary.

For compost in the vegetable garden, the methods and quantities to be used usually do not differ from those already seen for the garden. The valuable material is very suitable for plants that require a lot of organic matter, such as tomatoes, eggplants, pumpkins and zucchini, cucumbers, artichokes, etc., but it should be used sparingly (as indeed are all fertilizers) for all those plants, such as lettuce, chicory and radicchio, of which the leaves are consumed: the substances absorbed in excess accumulate precisely in the leaves and in some cases (such as nitrates) can be potentially harmful to our health. Its use is also recommended for the vegetable garden before the resumption of spring activities, but for more demanding plants it can also be used as a "reinforcement" for ongoing crops, burying a few handfuls per square yard not too deeply so as not to damage the plants.

Distribution instructions

- **Orchard:** After harvest, spread 1-2 lb/sq yd of mature compost in a layer up to 1 in thick over the entire area covered by the canopy.

- **Vegetable garden:** Depending on whether the vegetables are weak (spinach, valerian, chicory, carrots, onions, leeks, peas, beans), medium (salads, fennel, chard, parsley) or strong (tomatoes, squash, potato, cabbage, celery, asparagus) consumers of compost, 1-2 lb to 3-5 lb/sq yd is needed. Smaller doses are for mature compost, and way up for ready compost and fresh.

- **Tree and shrub planting:** 2-3 lb/bucket of ready compost for plants with a soil loaf; or the amount of mature compost needed to cover the root system for bare-root plants.

- **Flowerbeds**: 2-3 lb/sq yd of mature compost.

- **Roses and rose gardens:** After winter pruning, tamp down with mature compost.

- **Turfgrasses:** In reseeding or infilling degraded lawns, spread 1-2 lb/sq yd of mature compost over the entire surface in a 1 in layer.

- **Garden and balcony plants:** Add 30-70% (by volume) mature compost to the substrate already used.

How To Store Compost

Compost is a living organism composed of microbiological organisms and bacteria that require aeration, moisture, and food. It is simple to learn how to store compost, and putting it on the ground can boost nutrients. If you make so much compost that you can't use it right away, you can store it in a compost bin. Keep an eye on the moisture level when maintaining compost since it can mildew if it becomes too wet, but it should also not dry out completely.

Any good gardener makes preparations ahead of time. This might mean that your compost for the next year is finished before you put it down. This includes keeping the compost moist and nutrient-rich for the next season. By covering it with a tarp or plastic sheeting, compost may be readily kept on the ground. This keeps excess moisture from rain and snow runoff out of the pile while yet allowing some moisture to permeate and keep it moist. Worms that enter the pile and leave behind rich castings are a bonus.

When determining how to store completed compost, space is a crucial consideration. Composting on the ground is ugly and takes up valuable garden space, which many home gardeners do not have. You can keep the compost moist and churned by using your compost bin, but many of us have a continuous batch of compost going on, and the bin is essential for the next generation of rich soil conditioners. In this case, you may either store the compost in plastic bags or in a few cheap rubbish cans. For the best results, check the moisture levels in the compost and mix to bring the moist bottom layer into the dry top layer. Using a garden fork, turn the batch. If the compost is similarly dry, spray it gently and stir it. Compost should be utilized as soon as possible. The longer it is stored, the more nutrients it is likely to lose. Compost may be stored until the next season, but it must be used before then. If you store additional "food" for a longer amount of time or combine it with a nearly finished batch of compost, you can add it to the pile. This will increase the number of organisms in the compost and keep it alive.

Compost Tea

I've been using a tried-and-true method to increase harvests in my garden without resorting to costly fertilizers for the past few seasons. Fermented tea is a nutrient-rich liquid infusion that can be made by composting tea leaves. Making tea compost is a breeze, and you may use whatever kind of organic compost you like, whether it's homegrown or bought from a store. One might think of tea compost as a probiotic and multivitamin for plants. Extract (thus the term "tea") prepared from compost and water, compost tea includes nutrients and beneficial microbes that encourage plant growth and guard against pests and illnesses. I've done a little bit of writing about soil-based probiotics, which are gaining in popularity as people learn that they can provide a healthy dose of naturally occurring beneficial bacteria to supplement their meals. Many people, however, are unaware of the diversity of soil bacteria or that we may aid them through simple practices like tea composting. The benefits to the crop from this cheap and easy-to-make fertilizer are substantial.

All the benefits:

- **It helps plants grow faster.** Tea compost provides nutrients for the plant and the soil, leading to faster growth for the plant, a sturdier plant, and a better harvest. Over time, natural methods such as tea compost also help nourish the soil so that the benefits add up year after year.

- **It is a good alternative to toxic chemicals for the garden.** Tea compost can help plants resist diseases and pests more effectively and can replace toxic fertilizers, pesticides and herbicides. Tea compost is also a less expensive alternative to harmful garden chemicals and is not dangerous to pets, wildlife or insects.

- **It offers microbial protection from disease.** Just as with humans, the right balance of beneficial bacteria can help plants resist disease and fungi making them less susceptible to pests. The microorganisms in te compost compete with harmful microbes help plants gain an advantage against these pests.

- **It provides nutrients and beneficial organisms.** As I mentioned earlier, tea compost is essentially a probiotic for plants, providing a concentrate of the organisms plants need for optimal growth and improving nutrient levels and the soil microbiome.

How to make compost tea

Ingredients:

- 2 cups homemade compost (ensure thorough composting—it should smell pleasantly earthy) or organic compost purchased
- 1 gallon pure, filtered water

Instructions:

1) Combine the water and compost in a container or jar and keep away from direct heat or cold sources (I store it in my garage).
2) 2. Leave it for at least 5 days, stirring once a day.
3) 3. Drain the solids and irrigate the garden with the liquid.

Expert advice

This recipe does not require precise proportions, and a simple 8:1 water-to-compost ratio will suffice (or any higher ratio of compost). On reality, tea compost may be simply prepared and utilized in the garden in a huge five-gallon bucket. If you have a big garden, you can prepare enough tea compost in a 40- or 50-gallon barrel to cover the entire area.

Because compost contains a variety of microorganisms, it is critical to ensure that the compost you use has been properly decomposed and does not include pathogenic or hazardous germs.

If you build your own compost, make sure it has been at least a year or has achieved a temperature of at least 150 degrees for many days. The majority of store-bought organic compost was created using the right composting technique.

Before applying the final tea compost on plants, ensure sure there is no unpleasant odor or froth that might indicate the existence of hazardous bacteria. I use tea compost during the start of the growing season, when the plants have settled, and just before harvest.

How To Use Compost Tea

The best time to administer compost tea is in the morning, when the plants' stoma are open and the sun will dry the leaves and avoid fungal problems caused by excess moisture. If you are using the product as a wetter, apply it while the soil is damp. Spray most attractive plants in late winter to early spring, and then again when the leaf buds burst. Use tea before planting annual beds to boost beneficial microorganisms. If you have fungal or bug issues, use tea immediately and during each normal watering cycle. Compost tea is beneficial to houseplants as well. During regular watering times, use thoroughly diluted by at least half.

An important initial step is to prepare the right blend of compost and water. Compost tea can "ferment" in either an aerobic or anaerobic environment. Unaerated tea is combined with water in a container and fermented for 5 to 8 days. Teas that have been aerated are ready in 24 to 48 hours. You may manufacture them by draping a burlap bag over a container and saturating it with water, allowing the leached solution to drop into the container. Mixture can be sprinkled on plant leaves or soaked into the soil around the root zone. Teas can be used in their whole or diluted at a 10:1 ratio. When utilizing fertilizer to drench roots, use 5 to 10 gallons per 14 acre for bigger circumstances (approximately 19 to 38 gallons per.10 acre). Foliar sprays for big areas should be applied at a rate of 5 gallons per 2 acres (about 19 liters per 81 acres).

HOW TO SPEED UP THE COMPOSTING PROCESS

Problems with a slow-rotting compost pile: what to do about it? To ensure that all of the organic waste has a chance to decompose into humus in a calm and orderly fashion, you should start a second compost heap specifically for yard trimmings and uneaten fruit and vegetable scraps. However, if you just have access to a single compost container, you might employ a strategy that can hasten the process. You don't need to buy a commercial compost accelerator or a plastic rapid composter to get things going with the decomposition process. To hasten decomposition, have the compost pile collapse, and obtain humus-rich soil sooner, simply inoculate it with a natural homemade solution. In order to accomplish your goal, you need:

- 2 gal of lukewarm water
- 1 lb sugar or 1 cup molasses
- 7 oz of worm humus and/or 1 cube of brewer's yeast

Tip: Instead of commercial yeast and warm water, you can also use homemade wild yeast. Since it is less concentrated, it is recommended to use double the amount, i.e., about three or four gallons.

How To Prepare & Use The Compost Accelerator

Making a compost accelerator is quite simple:

1) Fill a bucket with warm, chlorine-free water and add the yeast cube or fresh worm humus.
2) Stir the water well to let the air in.
3) At this point, add the sugar and molasses and stir the mixture until the sugar is completely dissolved.
4) Set aside the mixture for about an hour. Occasionally stir during this process.
5) Now apply the finished compost accelerator evenly to your compost pile with a watering can and mix well.

6) The compost pile's temperature should climb during the next three days. (A compost thermometer is recommended if you wish to track the temperature curve.)

7) After about a week, flip or thoroughly mix the compost pile. There is no need to apply compost accelerator again.

8) The compost pile re-heats and can be utilized again 7 days after the last stirring.

How The DIY Compost Accelerator Works

Microorganisms, bacteria, fungi, and even larger creatures like worms all play a role in the decomposition of compostable trash. Compost microbes "work their way up" the compost bin's layers of plant waste as more garbage is added. Decomposition is hastened by yeast fungus, which are transported to the proper location via irrigation water and swiftly grow once they arrive. Microorganisms thrive in a sugar-and-water environment. A wet, warm, and airy setting is also beneficial for quick decomposition. For this reason, appropriate compost pile construction and upkeep is crucial. Composting that is "good," or aerobic takes place in conditions that are moist (80%), warm (>60°F), and aerated (aerobic). Bacteria and fungus thrive in these circumstances for rapid multiplication. The ratio of nitrogen to carbon should be around 1:20, as this is the energy ratio required. Compost accelerators are a convenient short-cut to achieving these conditions when one or more is lacking.

Advice: If you have worm compost on your balcony, you can use the fresh worm humus to speed up your compost pile. A wide variety of decomposer bacteria can be found in soil. Substitute 200 grams of worm humus for the yeast and add it to the water. Together, the compost and the heated, dissolved sugar, create the perfect environment for bacterial growth.

The worm humus then rapidly multiplies the beneficial bacteria and fungi, which start breaking down the biomass. As a backup option for introducing decomposer fungus, yeast works well. With the help of molasses, we can generate enough heat to keep the compost pile at an appropriate temperature (hot decomposition). A compost pile of at least 1 m3 in volume, but still heaped loosely, will allow for efficient drainage during heat decomposition. Within 24 to 72 hours of application, hot rotting will kill off most of the fungus spores and weed seeds. The maturity phase, in which the compost's nutrients are bonded, comes after the heat rotting phase. Less effort is needed at this point.

Proper Usage

It is recommended that compost accelerator be applied with a watering can. This will ensure an even application. Ideally, it is a dry day, not too sunny and with temperatures around 70°F.

- Pour the liquid evenly over the compost pile.
- Stir thoroughly

Now you have to wait and see. Over the next three days, the temperature of the compost heap should rise. For a layman, this warm rot is difficult to assess, so it may be useful to consult a special compost thermometer from the specialized industry. One week after application, the compost pile is mixed thoroughly again and/or, if necessary, moved. The time required to use the humus depends on several factors:

- Moisture
- Degree of comminution
- Material
- Temperature
- Composition of the waste

However, it is generally believed that fantastic humus is formed after about eight to ten months. Also, plants such as valerian, comfrey, nettle or fern fronds can also accelerate compost. They should be put with water so that they ferment. After the fermentation process, mix them with water in a ratio of 1:10 and add the solution to the compost.

idea
changes
objective act
teamwork goal
BUSINESS
marketing time
strategy key
success

MAKE MONEY WITH COMPOST

A composting business contributes to a tidy neighborhood by recycling organic waste such as leaves. This resource is transformed into compost, which has several potential applications including commercial and domestic use. Most businesses that deal with composting do it out of a sizable facility. They may charge a fee to collect other people's compost or to accept home deliveries. With the expanding market for green products and services, many individuals are beginning to reconsider waste. As a result, composting is no longer a rural waste disposal strategy. It is becoming more widespread as a method of controlling trash and producing a usable product—creating a viable business opportunity. A composting business could be ideal if you want to create an environmentally friendly business with high growth potential. In this chapter, we will find out how to start your own composting business and whether it is right for you.

The Benefits Of Composting Business:

- The most obvious advantage of beginning a composting business is that you are simultaneously helping the environment while striving to build your business. Composting is the process of reusing materials and keeping them out of landfills. Composting is one of the goals of finding easier and more efficient ways to recycle our materials, which is vital to sustainable living.

- **It is relatively simple to start a composting business. The startup costs are low.** Personal compost piles can be easily created by amateurs and enthusiasts, and there are no major impediments to spreading these do-it-yourself operations to a wider audience. There will be logistical challenges, but the firm can be launched. In contrast to other sorts of enterprises, you can start a composting operation in your own house, at least at first. From there, you can concentrate on expanding your local business or use the Internet to reach out to faraway customers.

- **Another advantage, in terms of customers, is the ease with which you can select target markets.** Composting organic material is in high demand, in addition to the increased demand for sustainable businesses. Compost is used by garden supply businesses, landscaping companies, and both professional and amateur gardeners to maintain their gardens healthy. Consumers will pay you to compost their garbage, and you can sell the decomposed material to various customers who will utilize it in their gardens.

- **You may be eligible for tax breaks for running a green business if you endeavor to minimize trash and promote recycling.** Composting alone, however, may not provide considerable tax savings. Although tax restrictions differ by state, the most popular tax credits are for green energy, energy-efficient building design, and fuel-efficient transportation, all of which could be incorporated into a composting operation but are not necessarily inextricably related.

The Disadvantages Of Composting Business:

- Although it is reasonably simple to start a composting business, sufficient land and space are required to construct a commercial composting site. Having enough room at the composting site is essential for growing the composting business. This could necessitate a considerable expenditure. You may also need to invest in equipment such as a delivery vehicle and compost storage bins.

- **Deliveries and shipping are also difficult.** Customers' waste must be collected for compost piles, and compost must be provided to customers who choose to purchase it. This causes logistical issues for transporting the substance. This is complicated by the fact that the raw composted material is essentially someone's waste.

- **Scientific knowledge, training, and physical ability are essential for the real labor.** You must grasp how to break down waste in a compost pile and how to achieve the best nutrient mix in the finished product. However, knowledge alone is insufficient, which is where training comes in. Before you can expect composting to be successful, you must first obtain a good understanding of composting through experience. As you gain experience, you rapidly realize the need of a strong back and stamina. Composting necessitates some elbow grease, and if you are unable to work long hours to construct compost piles, you will need to arrange to hire people who are.

How to Start Your Composting Business

1) Plan your business

An entrepreneur's success is dependent on having a well-defined plan. It will assist you in defining the characteristics of your business and revealing some unknowns. Consider the following crucial topics:

- What are the initial and ongoing costs?
- Who is your intended audience?
- How much money may you charge your customers?

Fortunately, I have done a lot of the heavy-lifting for you.

How much does it cost to start a composting business? This is a labor-intensive business that might be expensive to establish. Start-up expenditures can reach $1 million due to the cost of land and upkeep, the cost of shipping and distributing compost, and collection (if the business offers collection services). The majority of the costs are related to the land required for composting, maintenance tools, compliance with municipal and state standards, and vehicles to transport the compost to and from the site.

What are the hard costs of running a composting business? Gasoline for the trucks, marketing, office utilities, and personnel expenditures to manage the compost fields are ongoing expenses for this type of business. These expenses can run anywhere from $10,000 for a small composting field to hundreds of thousands of dollars for a large-scale enterprise.

Who is the intended audience? Local governments, HOA districts, farms, and commercial businesses that require a large amount of land are among the target markets.

How can a compost business make money? Composting businesses profit from the sale of fully composted material, which is essentially high-quality topsoil or "top soil" used as fertilizer or ground cover. It is often high in nutrients and is good for usage in farms, gardens, and residential areas.

What is the maximum amount that customers can be charged? It is determined by the local market. Selling in bulk increases total revenue but reduces profit margins. Companies often charge between $5 and $10 per cubic yard. Discounted prices, on the other hand, can bring these prices down to $1 or $3 per cubic yard. Local governments, as well as farmers that buy compost in bulk, can charge a lower price. A minimum charge of $1 per cubic yard is to be expected, with a selling price of $3 per cubic yard on average.

What kind of profit can a compost business make? Profit is mostly determined by local compost demand. Compost demand is high in some locations, allowing enterprises to generate net profit margins of more than 10%, while margins are quite low in others. For a small to medium-sized compost company, the average turnover in this (still young) industry varies from $500,000 to more than $1 million.

How can the company become more profitable? Making the firm more profitable is not an easy task. The primary method of increasing earnings is to reduce costs. However, finding cheaper sources for compost basic ingredients and lowering shipping costs are required. Buying land in low-cost, low-tax areas will boost profitability.

2) Choose a location

The restrictions imposed by rules will have a big impact on your site. A land may appear to be ideal, but if a neighbor's house is nearby or there is a stream running through it, your prospective processing area may be insufficient. Before you waste time visiting all of them, use Google Earth to eliminate unwanted properties. Of course, you want a property that is as close to your clients as feasible, but not so close that it is unreasonably expensive or causes complaints from neighbors. Money will fly out the door once the property is chosen, purchased, or rented. You must prepare it and obtain permits as quickly as possible so that you can begin earning money. Prior to the purchase, you must secure as many contractors as possible and complete the majority of the permits process. Then the countdown to opening day begins!

Grading, roads, and surfaces are the most significant aspects of site preparation. The location for food waste collection and initial treatment will require an impermeable surface, such as concrete (expensive) or asphalt (also expensive, but less so). Storage of shavings and leaves, as well as compost drying, can most likely be done on bare, reasonably level ground, but verify current restrictions. If there is already a composting facility nearby, you must establish the feasibility of adding another facility during the prelaunch assessment phase. You can be competitive if you have access to adequate raw materials and differentiate your firm through price or some aspect of the disposal service or completed product. It will, however, be more challenging. There are several locations where there are no plants at all. The major goal of my website and this essay is to expand the geographical reach of composting services and products into new locations.

3) **Find sources of organic waste**

To get your new compost company up and running, you'll need a consistent source of animal feces. The large composting monster in my region was built near a racetrack with horses all year. Then you'll need a consistent supply of other "feed material," such as leaves, ground trees, or even garbage from breweries and soda bottling factories. To keep the compost uniform, machines will be required to turn it every 3-4 days. You'll also need customers who want your compost, of course. It is also vital to check and secure all of the permits and licenses required for the firm. There may be issues if you do not have licenses and permits that conform with the regulations in effect at your facilities. Heavy fines and the closure of the business are among the issues. Using a personal delivery service with a large truck without a permission for the route, for example, can land you in hot water. Certificate of occupancy, state and municipal licensing requirements are just a few of the concerns to consider.

4) <u>Choose a composting method and build your farm</u>

Always begin with a large supply of dry charcoal. Wet nitrogenous material, on the other hand, cannot be hoarded because it stinks and attracts flies. Begin with two parts carbon and one part nitrogen and watch how it goes. Changes can be made from there, such as adding extra carbon or nitrogen. If the pile does not flare up but smells and attracts flies, there is too much nitrogen present. Increase the amount of carbon. It is preferable to add extra nitrogen if it heats up and does not stink but works too slowly. In any event, you must continue to experiment until you find the proper amounts. Composting is an art, and like any skill, it can only be learned through practice. I feel it is critical to keep things simple, efficient, and cost-effective. Before using windrow turners or pricey tank approaches, try static piles. It is preferable to study nature. Do what it has done well since the beginning. The static heap is extremely efficient. There is very minimal moisture waste.

Our piles range in height from 10 to 12 feet. They can absorb our yearly rainfall of 29 inches without losing moisture at the bottom. After heavy rains, we normally turn the piles over. The compost warms up and evaporates extra moisture, preparing it for the next rain. We almost never have to water our compost piles. Because the enormous size keeps the moisture in the compost material, we don't even need to water the pile when it's first formed. If the components are dry at first, they must be wetted while being ground or combined. A very dry heap cannot be thoroughly moistened from above. Water flows straight down and settles on the earth because there is no capillary attraction.

5) **Sell your product**

Once you've established an approximate launch date, you'll need to begin marketing your facility as a cost-effective disposal option and a source of compost. Do not wait till the preceding phase is complete before knocking on doors and gathering customers. If social media is not your strong suit, you should learn at least the basics of Facebook and Instagram. I'm not excellent at posting on a regular basis, but these platforms offer a cheap method to spread the word. Acquaint yourself with various types of articles, stories, and advertisements throughout time. Other platforms worth investigating include Pinterest and NextDoor.

Another approach to reach out to individuals is to speak at civic group meetings: Kiwanis, Rotary, and so on are good, but garden clubs are far superior. You'd be astonished at how many garden clubs there are. They are well-versed in the benefits of compost and the composting process. They frequently generate on their own, but they require much more. When promoting, whether in groups or online, attempt to collect as much contact information as possible so that you may contact them when you launch your composting company. Spend no money on print or radio advertising. I've spent thousands of dollars on these initiatives with no results. The same is true for direct mail. Furthermore, I've had very few responses by leaving flyers on people's doorsteps, which takes a long time. Finally. Your facility is complete, and you are permitted to operate. To begin your composting business, contact all individuals, businesses, and organizations who have expressed an interest in your services and products directly. Request that they sign up for your service. Use social media to let everyone know you're available. Request that everyone share your message and help spread the word.

Composting has numerous environmental benefits, including food recycling, lower landfill emissions, and less reliance on chemical fertilizers. As more individuals become aware of the benefits, the sector is rapidly expanding. Starting a composting business needs an investment and some hard work, but with genuine dedication and an eco-conscious mindset, you can create a profitable green business! After you've finished your homework, it's time to roll up your sleeves and start your lucrative composting business.

TROUBLESHOOTING

Compost is the foundation of a healthy garden. The issue is that few of us have the optimum conditions to make great compost all of the time. The ideal compost has a fine, granular texture and a nice, earthy odor reminiscent of forest soil. The original compost ingredients will be no longer visible, having been turned into dark-looking organic matter with a homogeneous texture. Gardeners love mature compost. Use it to mulch plants, prepare potting soils, or dig into the soil to boost nutritional content and moisture retention. In this final chapter, we'll look at some frequent compost issues and the simplest solutions to them.

My Compost Is Too Wet

Excess moisture is the most common issue, causing foul odors, insects, and the creation of plant-damaging chemicals. The usual culprit is the inclusion of too much fresh material rather than a balanced mixing of fresh and dry ingredients.

Fresh materials, such as vegetable peels and grass clippings, are heavy due to their high water content. When too much is added to the compost bin at once, it might become compacted, excluding air or filling air holes with water. These "anaerobic," oxygen-deprived conditions promote the growth of dangerous microorganisms, which are also responsible for the foul aromas produced by these putrid circumstances. Because fresh materials are largely "green," and have a high nitrogen content, mixing them with more carbon-rich "browns" will help fix the problem. If your compost bin is excessively damp, totally empty it and turn the materials to absorb more air before stacking them again. Add dry materials to the mix to achieve a green-brown balance, enhance drainage, and keep the compost from clogging again.

Composting ingredients such as shredded prunings, sawdust, straw, and shredded cardboard form channels inside the compost, allowing air to percolate and excess moisture to drain away. If you don't have enough dry ingredients on hand, rolled newspapers are an excellent short-term solution.

My Compost Is Too Dry

Decomposition will halt if the compost heap becomes too dry because the bacteria and fungus responsible for composting are unable to operate properly. Water the compost heap again, preferably with rainwater, but if precipitation is scarce, plain water will suffice. Apply it evenly using a rosette-equipped watering can, mixing the components together if possible. Bins with an excess of dry materials can be improved by introducing a large amount of fresh material to balance the contents. Dig the compost bin, then add the fresh stuff and fill it. Alternatively, if you have two bins next to each other, mix the excess materials and water as you turn the materials from one to the other.

Leaf mold, a type of compost composed exclusively of fallen leaves, is an exception to the rule. It takes up to three years for leaf mold to fully mature before it is fit for use, at which point the leaves should no longer be visible.

My Compost Is Too Acid

Compost is inherently slightly acidic, but an excess of certain "wetter" elements can throw the balance off. This might cause the compost pile to smell and disintegrate slowly. Acidic components, such as citrus, can also contribute to an overly acidic compost heap. To neutralize the acidity, add handfuls of pulverized lime or wood ash to the mixture, as well as lots of "browns" if the compost heap is damp and other fresh, green material to resume the composting process.

My Compost Smells

An anaerobic compost pile smells like rotting eggs or decomposing vegetables. This signifies that there is insufficient oxygen to sustain aerobic microorganisms, and anaerobic microbes have taken over. Unfortunately, as a consequence, these emit hydrogen sulfide, which smells like rotten eggs. The remedy is straightforward: turn the pile over. Because the operation demands being near to the stinky heap, it might be unpleasant. But it's worthwhile. Rebuild the turned over pile on a scoop to promote airflow from bottom to top. Alternatively, place heavy sticks into the pile's middle to provide support. If the pile continues to return to anaerobic state, it is time to experiment with alternative ingredient ratios or composting approaches. Some approaches, such as tarp composting, prevent the improper items from accumulating and stinking up the environment. By putting the process underground, the trench composting method suffocates odors.

My Compost Is Not Aerated

As soil composting develops, the core of the heap may become oxygen-depleted. Moving the pile allows air to reach all areas. A pitchfork or a compost aerator, a tool built expressly for this activity, can be used to aerate compost piles on the ground. You can also use a broomstick, rebar, or a long-handled weeding tool to poke holes inside the pile. Every time you turn a compost bin (a rotating container), it is aerated, but you should not overfill it otherwise there will be no room for compost. There is no hard and fast rule regarding aeration frequency, but once or twice a week is usually sufficient.

My Compost Is Crawling With Insects

Bugs are little crustaceans that live off of decaying organic waste. If you turn over the top layer of your compost pile and find millions of little gray armadillo-like critters with seven pairs of legs each, you've found a nest of these insects. Pill bugs, in contrast to sowbugs, may roll into a ball when threatened, but otherwise, they are very similar. The insects will not harm your compost and will really help it break down. If not removed from the finished compost before spreading it in the garden, they might damage the tender roots and leaves of young plants like beans, beets, and others.

Compost piles are a popular hiding place for insects like ants and earwigs. They are mostly harmless, like beetles and insects, to the composting process, but their presence may indicate that the pile is decomposing slowly. Raise the compost pile's temperature to over 120 degrees Fahrenheit to get rid of the pests *(if you are unsure of the temperature of your pile, measure it with a compost thermometer or a regular meat thermometer wrapped in plastic).* In order to get the best results, you should water the mound thoroughly and turn it over. Add a nitrogen source such as blood meal, manure, or oyster shells if there are a lot of leaves or straw. As the temperature rises, the bugs will leave for cooler climes. You should rotate the pile at least once every two weeks, and more often if you can. However, if you plan on using the finished compost at a location near seedlings, you should consider the possibility that it may include insects. Are you going to have to do everything from scratch? No. In order to dry, spread the compost out in a thin layer on a tarp and place it in the sun. Insects are quickly disappearing.

Insect management in compost

The presence of insects is unavoidable when composting. It could occasionally involve massive swarms of insects. Understand the importance of bugs in compost, and how to welcome the good ones while minimizing the bad. Let's look at the various species that are typically discovered in compost and what to do about them.

Good insects: The beneficial isopods, commonly known as bugs, slugs, or mealybugs, are common residents of the composting zone. Slugs behave in the same way. The latter like moist, dark nooks where rotting plant materials can be found. Several varieties of flies and beetles, as well as their offspring, are transitory residents of the compost. Adult flies are constantly scouting the surroundings for possible food sources for the larvae. Small fruit flies and larger black soldier flies larvae are voracious consumers of "green" compost items such as coffee grounds and kitchen trash. All of these animals have gathered to feast on the damp, decomposing items you've prepared. As soon as you drop it, they might begin devouring it. The energetic motion of hungry insects, which dig tunnels as they feed, can assist aerate the material. In their eagerness to consume, they can even assist warm a frigid pile.

These animals will discover your compost on their own. Simply give them what they want, and they will proliferate. They enhance the populations of bacteria and fungi in the compost as they develop, consume, and excrete. Fungi and bacteria are necessary for the breakdown process and provide food for earthworms. Finally, insects in the vicinity of the bin can provide a great food source for birds. Wild birds linger in your densely populated garden, ready to assist you with summer pests. The highly nutritious grubs and insects recovered from the compost are a favorite of the chickens. So, to summarize, the insects beneficial to our compost are:

Insect 1: Black Soldier Flies

Insect 2: Isopods

Insect 3: Worms

Bad insects: Crowds of compost insects might be bothersome, not to the compost directly, but to you or your garden. If the compost pile is overflowing with fresh fruit and vegetable waste, swarms of fruit flies (vinegar fly, fungus gnat) can be vexing in the summer. House flies that feed on waste can visit your compost; house flies remove waste, but they can also spread disease and infiltrate homes. Slugs and bedbugs that live in the dark corners of the composting area may pass by your strawberry or lettuce bed. Ants and bees will occasionally inhabit a section of the compost pile. Ants and bees do not contribute to the decomposition process and can interfere with compost utilization. Furthermore, little beetles (larvae) may settle in the compost. The characteristic white larva, formed like the letter C, could be a young Scarabaeidae beetle. These white compost larvae have the potential to develop into beetles that feed on garden or lawn plants. Among the insects we do not want to find in our compost are:

Insect 1: Centipedes

Insect 2: Houseflies

Insect 3: Bees

Insect 4: Spider

Insect 5: Ants

My Compost Attracts Animals

Contrary to popular belief, animals including raccoons, opossums, dogs, skunks, rats, bears, and many others do not consume compost but rather destroy it to get to the fresh waste that has recently been buried. It's possible to discourage animals from digging through your compost pile for buried food scraps by mixing in some soil or wood ash before you bury it (in the heated core of the pile). Once these dumpster divers have established a routine of frequenting your compost pile in quest of a free meal, you'll want to construct or purchase a covered bin (ideally an above-ground model, for example the tumbler composter) to keep the waste pickers at away.

COMPOSTING FOR KIDS

Composting is a simple and enjoyable project for families to do together. It's a fantastic learning experience that helps your home garden while reducing waste sent to landfills. Composting is an educational opportunity masked as a fun project for kids.

One of the best aspects about composting for kids is that it is not a one-time event. Making composting part of your family's daily practice strengthens your bond with one another, your garden, and the environment. They also get to see the process from start to finish and how it affects the fruits and vegetables in your garden.

Composting can be taught to even the youngest children. It's a simple formula with lots of advantages.

It is never too early to start your children composting! Kids typically enjoy being outside and doing things that make them feel and appear mature, and segregating waste, managing how it is used, and understanding the importance of the job can be quite exciting.

Composting with children can provide them with excellent hands-on experience. Here are some of the most important things that children may learn through composting, particularly if they do it themselves:

- Understand the value of reusing and producing less garbage.
- Discover more about the environment.
- Learn about the various nutrients that each item can supply to the soil.
- Discover how the entire composting system works.
- Discover a variety of scientific facts.
- Recognize the environmental consequences of our actions.

- Understand more about green living and environmental awareness.

It is extremely simple to teach kids to compost. You only need to teach them the recipe and show them the components. The rest is packed with science lectures and surprising discoveries.

In one chapter of this book, I have listed all the materials you can compost and those you absolutely must avoid. If children can't remember everything you can tape a list to the refrigerator or maybe near where you keep the trash. That way the little ones will be more involved in this activity even if it's just when they throw something in the bin.

Composting is so simple that even a child can do it! It might be difficult to keep up with it at times, especially if you're busy or the weather isn't cooperating. Here are a few pointers to help you have a more successful composting experience:

- **Indoor composting:** using a container with a lid to keep garbage avoids the need to frequently go outside to the compost pile. A mason jar or a little plastic container old plastic container goes great, and they may be stored anywhere that is comfortable for you.
- **Mix layers:** putting too much of one thing on the pile (for example, inches and inches of grass clippings) without

mixing it up will not work. A fifty-fifty ratio of brown and green stuff is ideal.

- **Establish a routine:** make a plan with your children to maintain the compost pile. Making it a weekly occasion helps you remember to turn it over and enjoy quality time together.

Composting Projects For Kids

The trick to getting children's attention and involvement is to stimulate their curiosity by turning the process into a game.

The following projects aim first and foremost to entertain our children to trigger their natural curiosity. Thanks to this book you will be able to answer all their questions and describe in a simple and understandable way all the processes they will witness. And now let's have some fun!

Treasure hunts

Treasure hunts are great for kids, and occasionally you need help finding good brown matter for your compost pile. Create a scavenger hunt in your yard to acquire more items for your pile. They will also help us collect leaves and keep our garden tidy.

Dead leaves make excellent brown matter, so why not have some fun with them as they fall in autumn? Form mounds to jump into before adding them to the compost or see who can collect the most leaves.

Materials and equipment needed:

- Compost bin or compost pile
- Dead leaves

Mini plastic composter

This fun project involves using a plastic bottle as if it were a composter bin.

The special feature of this experiment is that the process can be watched day by day because of the transparency of the bottle. In addition, children independently will be able to add kitchen scraps and mix the elements inside.

Materials and equipment needed:

- clear plastic bottle
- fruit or vegetable peels
- Shredded paper
- Spray bottle
- A pair of scissors
- Plant saucer

Instructions

1) Rinse the bottle
2) Cut off the top of the bottle and make some holes on the bottom to help the drainage
3) Adding a layer of shredded paper

4) Spray some water in the bottle to moisten the paper, be careful not to get it too damp, the paper should be moist not wet

5) Add fruit or vegetable peels

6) Take the top of the bottle that you previously cut off and lay it upside down on the bottle

7) Place the bottle behind a window so that it receives sunlight

8) Stir the mixture and check that the mixture is moist on a daily basis

Build a worm farm

Worms are amazing, especially as a child. They wiggle and slither all over the place; how cool is that? Worms can also aid with composting. You can set up a worm farm for your children to manage.

Materials and equipment needed:

- Clear plastic container with lid
- Shredded paper
- Kitchen scraps
- A drill
- Worms (you can collect them in the garden with the kids or buy them at a fishing store)

Instructions

1) Choose a container that is at least 10 inches high, drilling holes in the bottom on the sides and on the lid, this will increase aeration and promote drainage of excess water.

2) Soak the paper in water after which wring it out

3) Place the torn paper in the bottom of the container until a "bed" of at least 4 to 5 inches is created

4) Add a handful of worms

5) Now you can add kitchen scraps. For the first 3 to 4 weeks, do not add more than one cup of scraps per week

CONCLUSION

Dear reader, our journey of discovery of compost has come to an end. Thank you for coming to the end in our "chat" about such a complex and articulate rapidly expanding world as composting. Throughout this guide we have seen what compost is, the chemistry behind it, how to compost through different methodologies, and even start a business. I hope you got to discover new things about composting and appreciated the tips and tactics scattered throughout the book. Composting is a habit that is not only profitable, fun and effective, but also extremely important for the environment. Rising GHG emissions are a significant contributor to climate change and global warming.

We can all help save the earth by pledging to lessen our environmental imprint. The seven billion people on Earth consume varied amounts of available resources. According to UN projections, the global population will reach 9.7 billion by 2050 and more than 11 billion by 2100. Increased population increases greenhouse gas emissions and depletes the planet's resources. Increased greenhouse gas emissions have a direct impact on global warming: they accelerate climate change, which will have serious consequences for our planet. As the world's population grows, technology advances, arable land shrinks, hectares and hectares of forests are lost each year, seas become increasingly polluted, and temperatures rise, it is difficult to reduce the ecological imprint. In a nutshell, it's not a pretty image. We can all help combat global warming by making climate-friendly choices in our daily lives. And composting is one of the most important practices for saving the planet.

If you enjoyed this guide, please feel free to leave honest feedback on amazon so that other readers can make a more informed choice.

Kindest,

Jacob A. Moore

www.ingramcontent.com/pod-product-compliance
Lightning Source LLC
LaVergne TN
LVHW010946260125
802189LV00003B/61